Subject: The artist's studio

Hi

A quick email to say thanks for the studio visit. It was good to hear your thoughts on the drawing. I think what you said is absolutely true. I guess all drawings pose that question, and in this case the question, "What is it that is being drawn?" is part of how looking at the picture is also its animation.

See you at Melbourne Uni next week.

Cheers
Tom

Subject: Pictures from early zoo

Dear 

Good to see you, albeit fleetingly, at the NGV last week. I wanted to get in touch about some research I'm doing at the State Library. I'm looking at the disparate histories of Royal Park, but my current research has come to focus on a set of images of the early zoo.

They are all images of the Native Encampment. I'm not sure if you would have come across this in your work — it was established in the early 1880s by the director of the zoo, Albert Le Souef (whose name you may know from the Board for the Protection of Aborigines from the same period).

I first encountered the Native Encampment in the first of the attached images, an engraving from 1882.

I found myself drawn to the images inside the mia mia. I wondered if they could be works by Barak, an idea that was fuelled by the discovery that Le Souef was a member of the BPA, and that, later in the decade, he organised for men from Coranderrk to come down to the zoo for boomerang throwing demonstrations (not sure if Barak was among them). He even had a hut from Coranderrk brought down as an exhibit entitled "Aboriginal vestige". (I checked those Charles Walter images of Coranderrk to see if I could identify its markings. It is possible it's the hut Simon Wonga lived in, but I can't be certain).

2863c

The photograph of the Encampment from 1889 (the second image attached) seems to dispel the idea that the figures inside the mia mia were painted by Barak. It's hard to make out the figures clearly in this photograph but I don't think they look like his work. At the same time, I also came across photographs of two paintings by Caroline Le Souef, the zoo director's wife. One is entitled "Native Fight". The other is entitled "Corroboree". Both are attached. They seem to be from the same period as the Native Encampment. I was struck by the similarity between the figures in these two paintings and the figures inside the mia mia in the photograph of the Native Encampment. Perhaps the pictures inside that mia mia were not painted by Barak, nor by any other Wurundjeri contemporary of his, but by the zoo director's wife?

I've ordered the original photographs from storage and can now access them in the Heritage Reading Room. If you have time in the next week or so to come up the road to have a look at them, it'd be great to hear your thoughts on all this.

I hope all goes well with you
Warm regards
Tom

Subject: drawing, and photograph

Dear ████████

I saw your work yesterday in at the NGV. The watercolour drawing is stunning. The rhythm of those figures dancing around that fire seems to articulate a memory which is not just visual, but physical, and heard — the sound of bodies who dance and sing and themselves enact memories. I often find myself wondering about your compulsion to make these pictures. I am trying to think of a less dry word than "necessary", but they seem necessary. They look like images that needed to be drawn. They seem compelled — by memory, and an insistence that these things occupied this place — just as the movement of those figures (and even that very idiosyncratic image of fire) looks like it is compelled, "called up", by sound and singing.

Yesterday I was emailed a photograph of the Native Encampment, which I have attached. It's the first photograph I've seen where the Encampment is inhabited by people. I wondered if the people in the photograph came from Coranderrk. Do you know any of the faces in this image?

I am curious to hear what you think.

Warm regards
Tom

Subject: Minutes

Dear [redacted]

I wanted to email you mainly to thank you for retrieving all those minute books of the Board of the Zoological and Acclimatisation Society. When we spoke on the phone you said you'd be curious to hear about anything I happen to find in those huge old books. So I'm reporting back, letting you know about the interesting things I stumbled across.

I spent most of yesterday looking through the minutes at the Public Records Office in Nth Melb. As I mentioned to you on the phone, I was looking for information about the Native Encampment, the ethnographic display which was established in the zoo during the 1880s. The Encampment is first mentioned in the Board's minutes in early 1882. Le Souef (the zoo's director) reports to the Board on 20 Feb: "...it is also intended shortly to construct in the Gardens an old Native Encampment such as the Blacks used to live in when the white men first arrived in the colony. The Council thinks this will be a matter of great interest to many who have never seen or heard of such a thing; it will be the more interesting, as every detail will be faithfully carried out, even to the old weapons and stone tomahawks".

There are various other mentions of the Encampment during 1882, but the most interesting parts are from later in the decade, when Le Souef reinvigorated the display in anticipation of overseas visitors coming to Victoria for the 1888 International Exhibition. This from the minutes to the last meeting in 1887: "It is also intended before the opening of the Exhibition to re-establish the native encampment in the gardens, as such an exhibit will be interesting to the many scientific men who will doubtless visit the colonies next year. All the details of the encampment of the Aborigines who possessed the country where Melbourne now stands when the white man first arrived will be faithfully carried out".

Le Souef reports on the progress on the Encampment at various meetings during 1888, but there is an odd syntax in all these reports. He almost always uses impersonal constructions, though on 30 July he adopts a more direct syntax: "I have created the Blacks' Camp and it looks very well indeed". The last bit of this July meeting is the most interesting. The Board adjourns to the zoo grounds to admire the spruced-up Native Encampment and then there is a vote of thanks for Le Souef's wife, Caroline, for her work in painting the new displays. This part of the minutes seems to confirm what I had suspected from studying a group of images in the State Library: that the Native Encampment was a simulation created by Le Souef and painted by

Caroline Le Souef. There is a photo in the Library's collection (from the album of an overseas visitor to the 1888 International Exhibition) which shows the Native Encampment and Caroline's painting work inside one of the mia mias. I have attached a detail which shows her painting slightly more clearly than the full picture.

Thank you again for bringing that material out of storage. It has been really helpful to my research. I have full transcripts of all the material in the minutes related to the Native Encampment and would be happy to email them to you if it would be useful for you, or as a resource for other researchers.

Warm regards
Tom

PS: I should also say that I came across lots of other very interesting odds and ends about the early zoo, particularly about the various trips that Le Souef's son Dudley made to other British imperial cities in Asia to exchange native animals for new exotic species to enhance the zoo's collection. There is also an amazing entry about an overnight fire in the reptile building (caused by the building's wood-fired heating system), detailing how the zoo's snakes were all burnt to death that night.

Subject: photos, studio

Hi

Thanks for the conversation around that drawing yesterday. It was good to hear your thoughts on it, and how it's starting to function as a space. I'm not sure quite how far to push the picture's negation of itself. There's a constant swinging between dispelling the image into the material surface of the drawing (saturating the image with the process of its coming into being), and reinstating or insisting upon the figurative presences in the work. I guess that's part of what compels both of us about pictures in general, though in this case it's also a question about how the fragments of the specific image I am working from (and its related histories) register themselves in the work.

I have already tried to make the shift you suggested on the extreme left of the picture, with some success (I think).

B t w were you in at all this morning? One of the windows was open and that storm had blown a whole lot of photographs off my desk (see little jpeg attached). I hope none of your work was damaged.

Hope to see you soon.

Cheers
Tom

Subject: BPA, fires, pictures

Hi ██████

Thank you for sending through the pdf of the honours thesis. I do feel slightly embarrassed that we have lived together for four years without me reading it.

It was interesting to read that work on the "Half-Caste Act". I now realise that while Le Souef was trying to create that display at the zoo, he was also part of the BPA, agitating for that Act, for stealing children; actively destroying the Aboriginal communities whose culture he was at the same time seeking to memorialise. I was trying to make sense of that in front my drawings yesterday. What are those surfaces I am drawing, those presences I am trying to re-present? Are they finally screens for something else, this other history, this moment when the legislated stealing began?

Also, I saw Tony after school when we were picking up the kids yesterday. He mentioned a friend of his who lost everything in the Kinglake bushfires. They have a young baby, which is the only reason they decided to leave when the fire was approaching. The baby saved them.

I also told Tony about going to Ben and Keren's wedding at the zoo on the day of those fires, and that moment about 20 minutes into the ceremony when the wind changed very dramatically and the temperature dropped from above 46 to the high 30s. It's terrible to think that it was precisely that wind change which

resulted in all those deaths around Kinglake. Did you end up telling Keren that the place at the zoo where their wedding happened was the place where Le Souef's ethnographic display used to be? For me two imaginary presences are now conjoined at that site: the Native Encampment, those painted figures dancing and fighting inside the mia mia; and the feeling of that temperature drop on my skin at the wedding as a mnemonic cue to the idea of those fires, turning around at that moment, that incredible heat. Odd that this conjoining is the space of an image (those dancing/fighting figures) and a space without an image (those bushfires are rare as contemporary disasters for the almost complete absence of photographs from within the event). I guess this lack of images is partly because the fire caused extreme conditions of invisibility (all those car crashes as people tried to escape, blindly driving into other cars or trees). But also because of the speed and all-enveloping nature of the fire (if you were close enough to the fire to be able to see, you were close enough to be killed by its radiant heat). It didn't allow the distance which vision normally gives us, to see disaster without being subject to it. It left an image-less space in its wake.

Am working at the State Library this arvo and will leave at about 5, so see you at home about 5.30.

Tom x

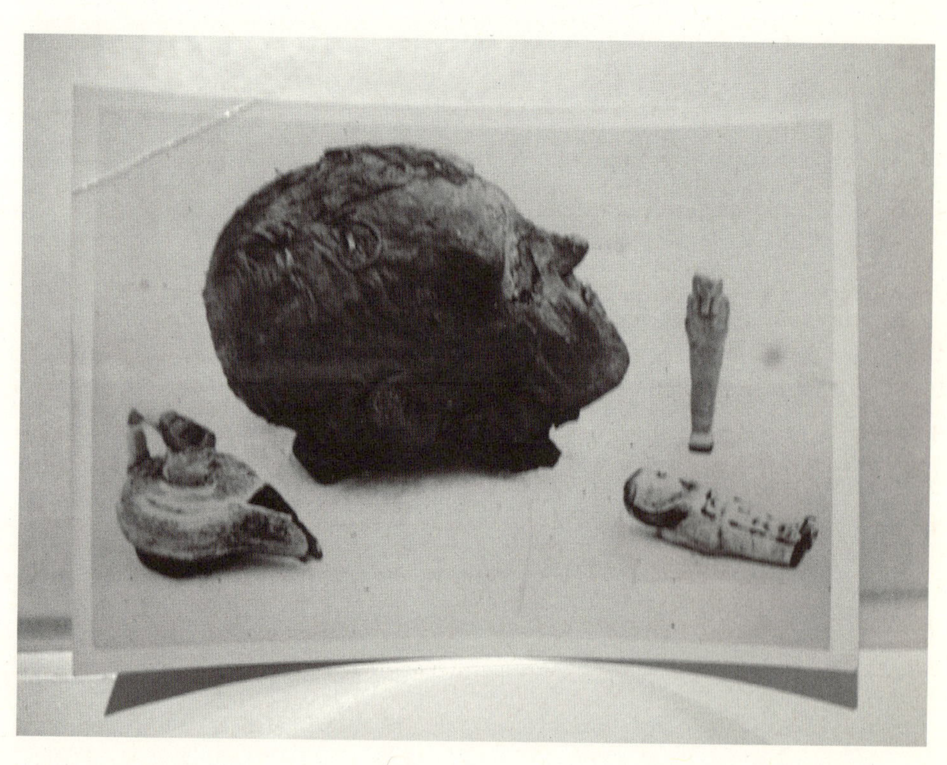

Subject: Sweet Damper and Gossip

Dear ███

Good to catch up with you at the Museum.

I chased up that Paul Fox essay on the Goulburn you mentioned. It's incredibly interesting. Not sure how much of it you remember, but he talks about Albert Le Souef a lot, particularly his experience growing up around the Goulburn in the 1840s, when his father William was the Protector there, and specifically when William tried to break up what he thought was a fight between neighbouring Aboriginal communities by firing shots into the air. It turns out the fighting was only pretend, a ritualised simulation of fighting which was part of the corroboree, part of the protocols of the two groups gathering. Apparently it was this, his father's confused impression, that Le Souef later described to his wife, which she faithfully painted in those two paintings — "Native Fight" and "Corroboree" — the ones I came across in the Le Souef family album in the State Library (the album I showed you two weeks ago which also had the photos of their living room in the house at the zoo, with all the Aboriginal and Papuan objects on the wall, and the photo of the mummified head he owned loose at the back. B t w, I forgot you wanted a copy of that photo and it is attached to this email). Caroline Le Souef's paintings on the inside of the mia mia in that photo of the Native Encampment are clearly

taken from the same two events, the fight and the corroboree, which were in actuality one and the same event. So the archaeology of her mia mia paintings is very odd indeed: simulations (of Aboriginal imagery); projections (based on her husband's oral accounts); projections (of Le Souef senior and his (mis-)understanding of what was going on that night near the Goulburn); simulations (as part of the corroboree, i.e. simulations of warring by the two Aboriginal communities). There is a blindness pervading all this, her picture-making. It feels odd to be drawing from an image of blindness. But this archaeology — her painting's archaeology of simulations and projections — is becoming the surface, and depth, of the drawing. Or I think it is. I don't know what presence it is invoking, what it is that is being drawn.

Also, it was good to do the zoo visit with the kids. The empty historical monkey enclosure was interesting to see, even if there is no sign whatsoever of the Encampment on the site where it used to be.

Cheers
Tom

Glossary of Names and Terms

Aborigines Protection Act 1886 was an act of the Victorian Parliament passed with the intention of merging a segment of the Aboriginal population with the general European population. Although in a national context the *Act* represented a radical shift in policy, it was consistent with attaining "finality", the objective held by the Board for the Protection of Aborigines (BPA), the colonial body charged with almost complete and unqualified jurisdiction over the lives of Aboriginal people by the *Aboriginal Protection Act* of 1869.[1] The 1886 *Act* was the first in Australia to attempt a "merging" and is regarded as the precursor to the national assimilation policies of the 1930s.[2] The *Act* worked to create distinctions between Aboriginal people based on the terms "full-blood" and "half-caste", and framed distinct regulations for each category. Aboriginal people of "mixed descent" were to be gradually incorporated into the white community and "full-blood" Aboriginal people allowed to die out in isolation on reserves and missions. In 1887, the BPA described the policy manifest in the *Aborigines Protection Act* as "the beginning of the end, which in the course of a few years will leave only a few pure blacks under the care of the Government".[3] Importantly, the Victorian *Aborigines Protection Act* functioned as a model for other states in Australia, with Queensland (1897), West Australia (1905), New South Wales (1909), South Australia (1910) and Northern Territory (1911) all passing similar legislation.[4] The 1886 *Act* can be considered the legislative origins of, and ideological codification for, the "stolen generations", the generations of Aboriginal people forcibly removed from their families as children under government policies.[5]

The important aspects of the 1886 *Act* were the provisions which drew a distinction within Aboriginal communities on the basis of descent, and because of this the *Act* became known as the "Half-Caste Act". The term "half-caste" was taken to mean "all persons whatever of mixed Aboriginal blood".[6] Under the *Act*, "half-castes" were to leave reserves within three years, but the BPA was to continue its "care and oversight" of "half-castes" for seven years after the commencement of the *Act*, controlling their place of residence, provision of supplies, apprenticeships and the institutionalisation of children.[7]

In effect, the *Act* forced members of Aboriginal communities off reserves and missions to find accommodation and employment in mainstream society.[8] It targeted a generation of literate Aboriginal people educated on missions whose political demands were creating "trouble" at missions such as Coranderrk.[9] The implementation of the *Act* saw the expulsion of about one-third of the adult population of the various reserves and missions operating in Victoria, and the removal of children from their families for "service with approved families", apprenticeships, or to orphanages.[10] The effects of the *Act* became an "important element of Aborigines' historical consciousness", and, even with the great hardships suffered in the era of the missions, made this missions era seem like a "golden age" by comparison.[11] At missions like Coranderrk and Lake Condah, Aboriginal resistance to the *Act* took various forms, informal and surreptitious means, as well as formalised methods, both of which are evident in the extensive correspondence records of the BPA following the implementation of the *Act*.[12]

The *Act* in part reflected a shift in the relationship between Aboriginal people and European society in Australia, "from one of exteriority to one of interiority".[13] As the process of colonisation unfolded, the frontier passed but Aboriginal people survived. The *Aborigines Protection Act*, with its elaborate racial schema, was part of a process of bringing Aboriginal people under control when there was no frontier separating Aboriginal and European, inside and outside. As Patrick Wolfe has written, "we find race intensifying when a social space becomes, or threatens to become, shared".[14]

Barak, William (c. 1824–1903), or Beruk, was a Wurundjeri Ngurungaeta (or headman) and artist. Born in the 1820s at Brushy Creek, near present-day Croydon, on the traditional lands of the Wurundjeri, he was the youngest of six children. His father was Bebejan, the Ngurungaeta of the Wurundjeri people, and his mother was Tooterie, of the Ngurailum balluk, the Murchison people, along the Goulburn River.[15] Barak was born approximately forty years after the beginning of the British invasion of the continent that became Australia, but it was only during his life-time that the effects of European presence began to be felt in his traditional lands, around the current site of the city of Melbourne. It is said that as a young boy he witnessed the meeting between his elders and John Batman, the entrepreneur and leader of the Port Philip Association. Batman's dubious "Treaty" with the Wurundjeri was the basis of his claim to 240,000 hectares of Wurundjeri land, and triggered the establishment of Melbourne. Barak lived through a rapid and violent process of dispossession, accelerated by the discovery of gold to the north of Melbourne in 1851. With the death of his cousin, Simon Wonga, in 1875, Barak became the Ngurungaeta, a role which involved extensive and difficult political negotiations

with the Crown. These were conducted largely through the Board for the Protection of Aborigines (BPA), the colonial body given jurisdiction over the lives of Aboriginal people by the *Aboriginal Protection Act* of 1869. From 1863 Barak and the Wurundjeri were based at Coranderrk, a mission station on the upper reaches of the Yarra River near present-day Healesville. Much of Barak's extensive political work as Ngurungaeta centred on Coranderrk and defending its autonomy.[16] Critical to this work was contesting the 1886 "Half-Caste Act", formally known as the *Aborigines Protection Act*, which created the terms for the forced dispersal of communities such as Coranderrk and the legislated stealing of children by the state.

It is not known when Barak began to produce paintings and drawings. His earliest works that can be confidently dated are from the early to mid 1880s.[17] In the body of work which survives, images of ceremonial practices and specific Wurundjeri historical events predominate.[18] With the exception of his painting, *Samuel de Pury's vineyard* (part homage, part satire on the vineyard and its geometrical incursion into the landscape), all of his surviving paintings take as their subject Wurundjeri culture and histories.[19] Much like his political work as Ngurungaeta, these images are powerful in part because of their insistence on the traditions of the Wurundjeri people, and their impicit claims to recognition and justice in the face of dispossession. Most striking in Barak's work are the distinctive pictorial rhythms, wherein forms are repeated and echoed and bodies patterned — or, in the case of his remarkable National Gallery of Victoria *Ceremony* watercolour, merged into single wave-forms running across the picture — to create powerful evocations of the sound, movements and singing of Wurundjeri ceremonies.[20] These pictorial rhythms figure dancing through drawing, and acutely link the mnemonic function of dancing in Wurundjeri culture to the function of drawing. The implicit political claims of the work — for the ongoing vitality and legitimacy of Wurundjeri culture — are lodged in this figuring of dancing through drawing, and in the visceral representation of collective practices and memory which would refuse the "finality" sought by colonial policy and the BPA.

Barak had three wives and was the father of three children. He outlived them all. His family lives on through the descendants of his nephew, Wandoon (Robert Wandin), the only surviving son of his sister Borate. Barak died at Coranderrk on 15 August 1903.

Black Saturday Bushfires were a set of bushfires which burned on and after 7 February 2009 around the state of Victoria. They were Australia's worst recorded natural disaster, with 173 people losing their lives, 7,562 people displaced, and 1.1 million acres burnt. The fires were precipitated in part by extreme weather conditions, culminating in temperatures in the mid-40s degrees Celcius. A cool change in the early evening on 7 February brought gale-force south-westerly winds of around 120km/h. In the case of the Kinglake Fire Complex, (a combination of the Kilmore East fire and the Murrindindi Mill fire), this wind change critically altered the fire's direction, causing the greatest loss of life as the fire front turned on communities like Kinglake West and Marysville. This fire burned for several weeks, threatening other communities around the upper reaches of the Yarra River such as Healesville. The intensity and speed of the Kinglake Fire Complex produced several firestorms and pyrocumulus systems, creating very low visibility and extreme levels of radiant heat. The amount of energy released during the firestorms in the Kinglake-Marysville area was equivalent to the amount of energy released by 1,500 Hiroshima-sized atomic bombs.

Board for the Protection of Aborigines (BPA) was a colonial body given almost complete and unqualified jurisdiction over the lives of Aboriginal people in Victoria, established through the *Aboriginal Protection Act* of 1869, the first comprehensive scheme to regulate the lives of Aboriginal people to be enacted in an Australian colony. Under this *Act*, the BPA was to control the residence, employment, marriage, social life and other aspects of daily life for all Aboriginal people in the Colony of Victoria. It was particularly powerful through its administration of the "Half-Caste Act", or the *Aborigines Protection Act* 1886, and the removal of Aboriginal children from their families. The BPA was replaced by the Aboriginal Welfare Board in 1957.

Centennial International Exhibition, Melbourne, 1888, was a major international exhibition held in the Royal Exhibition Building to commemorate the 100th anniversary of the British invasion in 1788. It was the last in a long line of exhibitions held in Melbourne during the second half of the 19th century, responding to the models of similar "universal" exhibitions in London and Paris. The first Melbourne Exhibition Building was opened in 1854, and reflected, along with the establishement of the University of Melbourne (1853), the Public Library (site granted in 1853) and the National Museum (1854), the wealth created by the Victorian goldrush and also an anxiety about the social chaos which accompanied it.[21] The first Melbourne Exhibition Building was situated on William Street (the site of the present Royal Mint) and housed both the 1854 Exhibition and the 1861 Victorian Exhibition.[22] A second exhibition building was erected in 1866 at the back of the Public Library and this building hosted the Intercolonial Exhibition of 1866, the Victorian Exhibition of 1872, and the Victorian Intercolonial Exhibition of 1875.[23] This building remained in use as

part of the Library and National Gallery complex until 1908, when it was demolished to allow construction of the Domed Reading Room, completed in 1913. By the 1870s, Melbourne was becoming a major city. In 1871 its population was 191,449; by 1891, it had reached 474,440, comparable with the great industrial cities of Europe.[24] This growth and wealth was reflected in the scale of the 1880 Melbourne International Exhibition and in the Royal Exhibition Building, constructed for this Exhibition in the Carlton Gardens, and later used to inaugurate Australia's Federation in 1901.[25] The 1880 Exhibition included exhibits from all the Australian colonies, as well as the United States and all the major industrialised countries of Western Europe. The Centennial International Exhibition of 1888 was held in the same building at an even larger scale, and attracted over 2 million visitors during 1888 and 1889.[26]

Coranderrk was a mission station on the upper reaches of the Yarra River near present-day Healesville, about 50 kilometres north-east of Melbourne. Coranderrk was granted to the Wurundjeri (and several other Aboriginal communities from different language groups) after a long and extensive process of lobbying by Aboriginal leaders and European sympathisers, such as the Presbyterian lay preacher John Green. The march of the Wurundjeri from Acheron, where they had been granted a temporary and infertile piece of land by the Crown, to Coranderrk, a site of traditional significance for the Wurundjeri, is celebrated in two remarkable images: a drawing by William Barak now held in the Ethnographic Museum in Berlin; and an 1865 photograph by the German-born photographer Charles Walter, in which this march is re-staged by the original participants.[27] These two images vouch for the importance of Coranderrk in the fight to maintain Aboriginal cultural, economic and political autonomy. Much of the political activism which emanated from Coranderrk, led by such figures as Simon Wonga and Barak, centred on Coranderrk and defending this autonomy.[28] Critical to this activism was contending with the 1886 "Half-Caste Act", formally known as *Aborigines Protection Act*. The communities at Coranderrk and other missions such as Lake Condah were active in contesting the *Act*, albeit unsuccessfully. The life of the community at Coranderrk is represented in a remarkable body of late-nineteenth-century photography, a medium which the Wurundjeri consciously adopted to press their claims for self-determination.[29] The mission was formally closed in 1924 and most residents were forced to move to Lake Tyers Mission. Five older people refused to move and continued living at Coranderrk until their deaths.

The Goulburn River is a major inland river in the state of Victoria. Originating in the Victorian Alps, it flows into the Murray River near the town of Echuca. The river is named after Henry Goulburn, a Conservative British Parliamentarian and militant Protestant who served as Chief Secretary for Ireland from 1821–1827.

Half-Caste Act (see Aborigines Protection Act)

Kinglake Bushfires (see Black Saturday Bushfires)

Le Souef, Albert Alexander Cochrane (1828–1902), a prominent figure in public life in the early history of Melbourne, led the early development of the Zoological and Acclimatisation Society of Victoria (now known as the Melbourne Zoo) between 1870 and 1902.[30] Born at Sandgate, Kent, England, but educated at the Moravian Mission School in Neuwied, Germany, he was 12 years old when his family emigrated to Melbourne in 1840. His father, William Le Souef, assumed the position of Protector of Aborigines on the Goulburn River in 1840 and Albert spent three years there on the protectorate station.[31] These three years proved formative. They shaped Albert's long-term membership of the Board for the Protection of Aborigines (BPA), his extensive collection of miniature Aboriginal weapons, and his activities as Secretary, then Director, of the Zoo (including the creation of the "Native Encampment", an ethnographic display he created at the Zoo in 1882, and boomerang events during the late 1880s, in which Aboriginal men from Coranderrk were brought to the Melbourne Zoo to perform public demonstrations of boomerang throwing). They also informed the creation of the *Le Souef Box*, a varnished wooden chest decorated with vignettes of Aboriginal life in the 1840s, now held in the collection of Museum Victoria and first exhibited at the 1866 Melbourne Intercolonial Exhibition.[32] Created by Le Souef and his wife Caroline, the box contains a set of miniaturised Aboriginal weapons carved by Albert, while the outside is decorated with detailed ink drawings made by Caroline. These depict scenes of life of the Taungurong people, indigenous to the Goulburn River region in Victoria, and were based on her husband's recollections of his childhood years there.[33]

Le Souef became Secretary of the Zoological and Acclimatisation Society of Victoria in 1870 and served as its Director from 1882 until 1902. During these thirty-two years of administration he was instrumental in the development of the early Zoo, increasingly moving the Zoo's activities away from its early mandate in the acclimatisation of exotic animals and towards the conception of the Zoo as a space of leisure and education.

From 1863 until 1893 Le Souef was Usher of the Black Rod in the Legislative Council of Victoria. He was a long-time member of the Board for the Protection of Aborigines (BPA) (from 1875 until his death in 1902,

including two periods as Vice-Chairman, 1879–81, 1896–99).[34] Through the BPA, he was also active in the enforcement of the 1886 *Aborigines Protection Act*. Le Souef was also a member of the Australasian Association for the Advancement of Science and a corresponding member of the Zoological Society, London.

In 1853 Le Souef married Caroline, born on 15 July 1834, in Barnstaple, Devon. Le Souef died at Royal Park on 7 May 1902 and was buried in Melbourne General Cemetery. His oldest son, Dudley, assumed his father's position as Director of the Zoo.

Le Souef, Caroline (1834–1915) was the wife of Albert A. C. Le Souef and an artist in her own right. She was the daughter of the pastoralist and naturalist John Cotton (1802–49), who emigrated to Australia with his wife Susannah and their nine children in 1843.[35] She married Le Souef in 1853 and for the majority of their married life they lived in the grounds of the Melbourne Zoo. Caroline was an artist, and two of her paintings, *Corroboree* and *Native Fight*, are held in the Museum Victoria collection. These two paintings and the ink painting decorating the outside of the *Le Souef Box*, were based on her husband's recollections of events of his childhood near the Goulburn River.[36] She died at Royal Park, Melbourne, on 8 March 1915. Three of her ten children became prominent in Australian zoological gardens. Her eldest son, Dudley Le Souef (1856–1923), took over the role of Director of the Melbourne Zoo upon his father's death in 1902, and was a prolific naturalist and ornithologist. Her second son, Ernest Le Souef (1869–1937), became the inaugural Director of the Perth Zoological Gardens in 1897. Her fourth son, Sherbourne Le Souef (1877–1951) was the first Director of the Taronga Park Zoo in Sydney.

Le Souef, Dudley (1856–1923) was the Director of the Zoological and Acclimatisation Society of Victoria, now known as the Melbourne Zoo, from 1902 until 1923. He was the eldest son of Albert A. C. Le Souef (1828–1902), who led the early development of the Zoo from 1870 until 1902, and Caroline Le Souef (1834–1915). Dudley was appointed Assistant-Secretary of the Zoo in 1874 at the age of 18, and in that capacity he made many collecting trips overseas between 1880 and 1888, visiting India, the United States, Singapore, Sumatra, England, Europe, Japan and New Guinea. He became Assistant Director in 1890 and, upon the death of his father in May 1902, assumed the position of Director, a position he held until his death in 1923.

Le Souef, William was the Protector of the Aborigines at the Goulburn River from 1840 to 1843, and the father of Albert A. C. Le Souef, the leading figure in the early development of the Melbourne Zoo. William arrived in Australia with his wife Ann and their children in 1840. His tenure as Protector of the Aborigines was marred by allegations that he was unfit for the position, allegations supported by George Augustus Robinson, the Chief Protector of the Aborigines, and Charles La Trobe, then Superintendent and later the first Governor of Victoria.[37] An inquiry held in 1843 found that Le Souef had embezzled funds and rations and misused Protectorate resources such as servants, land and equipment for his own profit. His activities as Protector are documented more favourably in his son Albert's unpublished *Personal Recollections of Early Australia*, and also informed Albert's interests in Aboriginal culture and his long-time involvement in the Board for the Protection of Aborigines (BPA).[38]

Melbourne Zoo is situated in Royal Park, in Melbourne's inner north, and was originally known as the Zoological and Acclimatisation Society of Victoria. It was established in 1862, and, like other Australian zoos in Sydney, Adelaide, and Perth, the Melbourne Zoo was initially charged with the "acclimatisation" of exotic species, regarded by colonial administrators as an important part of economic development in the new Colony of Victoria.[39] In the Pictures Collection of the State Library of Victoria there are numerous images which attest to this part of the early Zoo's mandate, chiefly showing different breeds of goats grazing in the open spaces of the Park. Over time, the acclimatisation mandate receded in importance and the Zoo's council focused its attention on the Zoo's development as a space of leisure and education. Indeed, as much as the idea of the Zoo was inherited from a set of imperial ideals, its layout was modeled after the London Zoo, and at first it was its formal gardens as much as its fairly paltry animal displays that attracted visitors. Zoos Victoria is the umbrella body which today manages the Melbourne Zoo, the Open Range Zoo at Werribee, and the Healesville Sanctuary, located on the upper reaches of the Yarra River.

Mia mia is a shelter built by Aboriginal people using wood, bark, branches and leaves.

Museum Victoria is the main public history and science museum in the state of Victoria. Currently situated in Carlton in inner Melbourne, it was originally founded in 1854 as the Museum of Natural and Economic Geology, with William Blandowski, the German-born zoologist, geologist, botanist and ethnologist, as the first scientist appointed to the staff. The Industrial and Technological Museum was established in 1870, initially built around material exhibited at the Melbourne Intercolonial Exhibition of 1866–67, and later parts of this collection were merged with the collection of the Museum. In 1899 the Museum moved from the University of Melbourne to its Swanston Street site, which it shared with the Public Library and the National Gallery. It was at this time that the the

prominent anthropologist and university administrator, Sir Baldwin Spencer, was appointed its Director. The Museum remained at its Swanston Street site until 2000, when it moved to its current site adjacent to the Royal Exhibition Building.

National Gallery of Victoria (NGV) is the major public collection of art in the state of Victoria. Founded in Melbourne in 1863, the Gallery developed out of the Public Library, and shared the Library's building on Swanston Street (along with its associated art school, the National Gallery School, founded in 1867) until it moved to a purpose-built building in the centre of Melbourne in 1968.[40]

Native Encampment was an ethnographic display at the Melbourne Zoo created in 1882 by the Zoo's Director, Albert A. C. Le Souef.[41] The display was renovated to coincide with the Centennial International Exhibition of 1888, in anticipation of the many visitors who would be drawn to Melbourne for the Exhibition.[42] It included mia mias, various weapons and carved objects and was situated near one of the Zoo's ponds, at the current site of the Zoo's function centre. In one photograph from 1888, the display is inhabited by Aboriginal men, women and children, probably brought to the Zoo from Coranderrk by Le Souef. Normally, though, the display was not inhabited.

North Melbourne is an inner-city suburb immediately to the north-west of the centre of Melbourne. The first state institutions were built in the area in the 1840s, though most of the suburb's architecture belongs to the era of the gold rush, from the 1850s until the 1880s.[43] Indeed, men and women arriving in Melbourne from around Ballarat and other goldfields would often enter the city through North Melbourne, and the suburb consequently developed a thriving range of pubs and brothels. The suburb lies adjacent to Royal Park, the vast park of Melbourne's inner north which also contains the Melbourne Zoo, the Royal Children's Hospital, and, historically, various national and international military camps. Recently institutions such as the Public Records Office of Victoria (PROV) and the National Archives of Australia have moved into North Melbourne.

Public Records Office of Victoria (PROV) is the archive of the State Government of Victoria. It holds records from the European settlement of Port Phillip District in the mid-1830s until today. Though it also has a Centre in Ballarat, its main site is in the inner Melbourne suburb of North Melbourne, where it shares a building with the National Archives of Australia Victorian State Office.

Royal Park is a vast park in Melbourne's inner north. In 1845, Governor Charles La Trobe set aside a reservation of more than 10 square kilometres for parkland and open space to the north of Melbourne's city centre. By the time of the Park's proclamation in 1854, its size had been reduced to just over six square kilometres. This was further reduced with the rapid increase of population from the Victorian gold rush and the formation of the suburb of Parkville, which today lies around the perimeter of the Park. The relocation of the Zoological and Acclimatisation Society of Victoria into the centre of Royal Park was just one of many incursions by the state. Others included: transport infrastructure (roads, a tramline and the Coburg railway line in 1885, now the Upfield Line); The University High School in 1929; The Royal Melbourne Hospital in 1944; The Royal Children's Hospital in 1957; the Royal Dental Hospital in 1963. Indeed, the history of the Park as a home for institutions of the state — as much as its odd appearance as a final vestige of complete wilderness at the edge of the city centre — is perhaps its defining characteristic. Royal Park is the only nineteenth-century park in Melbourne never to have been landscaped with exotics, a fact perhaps connected to its long history of military and large-scale ceremonial use. When the Duke of York visited Australia in 1901 to mark the nation's Federation and to open its first Parliament at the Royal Exhibition Building, he also watched military displays in Royal Park, including dancing and military drills by Fijian soldiers (an occasion recorded in two remarkable stereographs held in the State Library of Victoria).[44] Indeed, by virtue of its many uses by the state (and the necessity for these uses to be recorded and also disseminated as propaganda), Royal Park is well represented in the Pictures Collection of the State Library of Victoria and in other official archives and libraries, and these photographs are often patterned by the spectacle of bodies in military formations, dancing or simulating fighting.[45] Royal Park was used as an enrolment centre and military camp during World War I, and there are several remarkable photographs of soldiers posed before white tents in Royal Park held in the Pictures Collection of the Australian War Memorial in Canberra.[46] During World War II, Royal Park became Camp Pell, one of the largest military camps in the Pacific Conflict, housing thousands of US, British and Australasian troops. Following the conclusion of World War II, the wooden huts of Camp Pell were given over to emergency public housing and, often maligned as a "slum", Camp Pell became an ongoing source of public controversy. Camp Pell was cleared a few months before Melbourne hosted the 1956 Olympic Games, and Royal Park was returned to the vast open spaces which characterise the Park today.

State Library of Victoria is the major public library in the state of Victoria. Founded as the

Melbourne Public Library in 1853 by Governor Charles La Trobe, it opened in February 1856 at the site which it still occupies in central Melbourne. The ambition of the first chair of the Trustees, the Judge Redmond Barry, to make the Library "at least the second best in the world ... to the British Library" reflected the self-confidence but also the anxieties brought about by the economic growth of the gold rush.[47] The Library was one of several educational institutions established in 1850s Melbourne which were conceived as bulwarks against "ignorance and vice". To this end, Barry excluded from the initial collection books "usually classed as works of fiction and of the imagination".[48] By the 1880s the Library was the largest in the Australasian colonies and the size of its collection was comparable to the major public libraries in England. The construction of the vast Domed Reading Room, completed in 1913, made room for the growth of the collection and was also conceived as an act of emulation — and surpassing — in relation to the Reading Room in the British Museum in London. For many years, the Library shared a building with the National Gallery of Victoria and Museum Victoria, but is now the sole tenant of the building at its original site on the corner of Swanston and La Trobe Streets.

University of Melbourne is the oldest university in the state of Victoria, and was founded in 1853. It was built on a site set aside by Governor Charles La Trobe in Parkville, in Melbourne's inner north, a site which remains the University's principal campus today.[49]

Victoria is the second most populous state in Australia. It is named after Queen Victoria, who was the reigning British monarch when the state was formally established in 1851, and its capital city is Melbourne, Australia's second largest city, with a population of 4 million. Before the British invasion, the part of the continent that became Victoria was a dense patchwork of different Aboriginal societies, divided into 39 distinct language groups and organised into larger national polities. The British invasion of the continent first reached present-day Victoria in the form of fatal diseases, but British colonists themselves did not arrive in significant numbers until many decades after the establishment of Sydney in 1788. Although there were earlier (failed) attempts at small-scale settlements, it was the arrival of the entrepreneur John Batman and his Port Philip Association, and specifically Batman's dubious "Treaty" signed with Wurundjeri elders in 1835, which triggered the establishment of a settlement in the Port Philip District, subsequently the city of Melbourne. At first the Port Philip District was treated as part of the Colony of New South Wales (NSW) and came under the administration of the colonial government in Sydney. In 1851 a new colonial entity was created, the Colony of Victoria, encompassing the land south of the River Murray, with Charles La Trobe as its first Governor and Melbourne as its capital. The early development of the Colony was propelled by the discovery of gold north of Melbourne, which prompted an immense influx of immigrants from Europe, China, and other Australian colonies and dramatically intensified the process of dispossession and violence towards Aboriginal communities within the Colony. In 1901, upon Federation, Victoria became a state within the newly independent nation of Australia.

Walter, Charles (1831–1907) was a photographer active in the Colony of Victoria from the early 1860s.[50] He arrived in Victoria from Germany in 1855 and was a specimen collector for the botanist Ferdinand von Mueller by 1856.[51] His earliest known photographs are from 1862, and he has been described as "possibly Australia's first photojournalist".[52] His most significant photographs were taken at Coranderrk from 1865. His large-scale panel of 104 individual portraits of men, women and children from Coranderrk was exhibited at the 1866 Intercolonial Exhibition in Melbourne and is now held in the La Trobe Pictures Collection of the State Library of Victoria.[53]

Wonga, Simon (1820s–1875) was a Wurundjeri Ngurungaeta (or headman), and an important Aboriginal political leader at a period of rapid and violent dispossession in the Colony of Victoria. He was the son of Billebellary, an elder of the Wurundjeri, who in 1835 met John Batman, the entrepreneur whose dubious "Treaty" with the Wurundjeri was the basis of Batman's claim to 240,000 hectares of Wurundjeri land. Wonga assumed the role of Ngurungaeta in 1851, and was active in arguing for the rights of Aboriginal people at a time when the gold rush had radically accelerated the process of colonisation. In 1859, along with several Taungurong men from the Goulburn River, he lobbied the Assistant Protector William Thomas for land near the junction of the Goulburn and Acheron Rivers. In 1860, he lobbied successfully for a small amount of Wurundjeri ceremonial land, along the upper reaches of the Yarra River, near present-day Healesville. The mission station there came to be known as Coranderrk. Wonga died of tuberculosis in early 1875 at Coranderrk, and the role of Ngurungaeta was assumed by his cousin, William Barak.

Wurundjeri are the Aboriginal people indigenous to the land occupied by the city of Melbourne and the land to the north and east of Melbourne. They belong to the Woiwurrung language group and to the Kulin nation.

Zoological and Acclimatisation Society of Victoria (see Melbourne Zoo)

Notes to Glossary

1 *Board for the Protection of Aborigines in the Colony of Victoria, Resolutions, Minutes*, 2 July 1884, B314, Roll 1, National Archives of Australia, Melbourne; see also, Tony Birch, "Come and See the Giant Koala", *Meanjin*, 58, no. 3, 1999, p 72. For an analysis and history of the *Act*, see: Clare Land, *Shifting Definitions: The 1886 Aborigines Protection Act, 'race' and 'half-castes'*, unpublished honours thesis, University of Melbourne, 2001.

2 John Chesterman and Brian Galligan, *Citizens without rights: Aborigines and Australian Citizenship* (Cambridge; Melbourne: Cambridge University Press), 1997, p 20; Katherine Ellinghaus, "Regarding Koori Marriages: The 1886 Victorian Aborigines Protection Act", *Fresh Cuts – special issue of the Journal of Australian Studies*, 67, 2001, p 22; Land, *Shifting Definitions*, p 3; Patrick Wolfe, "Nation and Miscengenation: Discursive Continuity in the Post-Mabo Era", *Social Analyses (Adelaide)*, no. 36, 1994, p 101.

3 *Twenty-Third Report of the Board for the Protection of the Aborigines in the Colony of Victoria. Presented to Both Houses of Parliament* (Melbourne: Board for the Protection of Aborigines), 1887, p 4. For an analysis of the effects of assimilation in relation to more direct forms of violence, see Gary Foley, "Australia and the Holocaust: A Koori Perspective", *Gary Foley's Koori History Website*, http://www.kooriweb.org/foley/, 1997.

4 Richard Broome, *Aboriginal Australians: Black Responses to White Dominance*, 1788–1994, 2nd ed., *Australian Experience*, No. 4 (St. Leonards, NSW: Allen & Unwin), 1994, pp 97–98.

5 National Inquiry into the Separation of Aboriginal and Torres Strait Islander Children from their Families, *Bringing Them Home: Report of the National Inquiry into the Separation of Aboriginal and Torres Strait Islander Children from their Families* (Sydney: Human Rights and Equal Opportunity Commission), 1997.

6 *The Aborigines Protection Act*, 1886, 50 Victoriae, no. 912.

7 John McCorquodale and Australian Institute of Aboriginal Studies, *Aborigines and the Law: A Digest* (Canberra: Aboriginal Studies Press), 1987, p 82.

8 Land, *Shifting Definitions*, p 20.

9 M. F. Christie, *Aborigines in Colonial Victoria, 1835–86* (Sydney: Sydney University Press), 1979, pp 182–195.

10 *Twenty-Second Report of the Board for the Protection of the Aborigines in the Colony of Victoria. Presented to Both Houses of Parliament* (Melbourne: Board for the Protection of Aborigines), 1886, p 3; *Twenty-Sixth Report of the Board for the Protection of the Aborigines in the Colony of Victoria. Presented to Both Houses of Parliament* (Melbourne: Board for the Protection of Aborigines), 1890, p 3.

11 Christie, *Aborigines in Colonial Victoria*, pp 201–2. See also Diane Barwick, "Equity for Aborigines?: The Framlingham Case", in *A Just Society?: Essays on Equity in Australia*, ed. Patrick N. Troy (Sydney: George Allen & Unwin), 1981; Jan Critchett, *A History of Framlingham and Lake Condah Aboriginal Aboriginal Stations, 1860–1918*, unpublished M. A. University of Melbourne, 1981.

12 Penny van Toorn, "Hegemony or Hidden Transcripts?: Aboriginal Writings from Lake Condah, 1876–1907", *The UTS Review*, 7. No. 1, 2001, pp 44–58; Diane Barwick, *Rebellion at Coranderrk* (Canberra: Aboriginal History Inc.), 1998; National Inquiry into the Separation of Aboriginal and Torres Strait Islander Children from their Families, *Bringing Them Home*.

13 Patrick Wolfe, "Land, Labor, and Difference: Elementary Structures of Race", *The American Historical Review*, 106, no. 3, 2001, p 871.

14 Wolfe, "Land, Labor, and Difference", p 887.

15 Joy Murphy-Wandin, "Barak My Uncle", in Carol Cooper, Joy Murphy-Wandin and Judith Ryan, *Remembering Barak*, exh. cat. (Melbourne: National Gallery of Victoria), 2003, p 5.

16 See *Report of the Board Appointed to Enquire into, and Report upon, the Present Condition and Management of the Coranderrk Aboriginal Station, together with the minutes of evidence* (Melbourne: Government Printers), 1882; Barwick, *Rebellion at Coranderrk*; Jane Lydon, *Eye Contact* (Durham: Duke University Press), 2005.

17 Cooper, "Remembering Barak", p 22.

18 Judith Ryan, "Barak: A Singular Artist", in Cooper, Murphy-Wandin, and Ryan, *Remembering Barak*, pp 11–13.

19 Barak, *Samuel de Pury's vineyard*, watercolour, 56.0 × 76.0 cm, Musée d'Ethnographie, Neuchâtel.

20 For example, see Barak, *Ceremony* (late 1890s), pencil, wash, ground wash, charcoal solution, gouache and earth pigments on paper, 57.0 × 88.8 cm, Natonal Gallery of Victoria (reproduced in Andrew Sayers, *Aboriginal Artists of the Nineteenth Century* (Melbourne: Oxford University Press), 1991, p 24).

21 Ian Morrison, "'The Accompaniments of European Civilization': Melbourne Exhibitions 1854–1888", *The La Trobe Journal*, No 56 Spring 1995, p 6.

22 *Official catalogue of the Melbourne Exhibition 1854* (Melbourne: Sinnett), 1855; *Catalogue of the Victorian Exhibition* (Melbourne: John Ferres), 1861; and, *Catalogue of the Victorian Exhibition* (Melbourne: Gibbs, Shallard & Co.), 1861.

23 *Intercolonial Exhibition of Australasia, Melbourne 1866–67: official record* (Melbourne: Blundell), 1867; and, "Previous exhibitions", *Official record of the Centennial International Exhibition, Melbourne 1888–1889* (Melbourne: Sands & MacDougall), 1890, pp 124–127.

24 Morrison, "'The Accompaniments of European Civilization': Melbourne Exhibitions 1854–1888", p 8.

25 David Dunstan, *Victorian Icon: A History of the Royal Exhibition Building* (Melbourne, Exhibition Trustees), 1995; Graham Davison, "Festivals of Nationhood", in S.L. Goldberg & F.B. Smith (ed.), *Australian Cultural History* (Cambridge: Cambridge University Press), 1988; Paul Fox, "Exhibition City: Melbourne and the 1880 International Exhibition", *Transition: Discourse on Architecture*, 31, Summer 1990, pp 62–71.

26 *Official record of the Centennial International Exhibition, Melbourne 1888–1889* (Melbourne: Sands & MacDougall), 1890; Graham Davison, J.W. McCarty, A. McLeary (eds), *Australians 1888* (Broadway, NSW: Fairfax, Syme & Weldon), 1987, pp 21–27;

27 See Barak, *Ceremony ochres* (date unknown, probably early 1890s), pencil, 48.5 × 68.0 cm, Staatliche Museen Preußischer Kulturbesitz, Museum für Völkerkunde, Berlin; and, Charles Walter, *The Yarra Tribe starting for the Acheron 1862* (1865), albumen silver photograph, 14.5 × 17.6cm, La Trobe Picture Collection, State Library of Victoria, Melbourne. Barak's drawing was bought for the Berlin Ethnographic Museum by the amateur German ethnographer, Arthur Baessler, who travelled to Coranderrk in December 1892 and whose enthusiasm for Barak "der König" is described vividly in his book *Südsee Bilder* (Berlin: Reimer), 1895. A powerful analysis of these two images and their relationship to this critical event in Wurundjeri history is contained in Lydon's book *Eye Contact*,

pp 60–72, as well as in Carol Cooper's essay, "Remembering Barak", in Cooper, Murphy-Wandin, and Ryan, *Remembering Barak*, pp 29–35.

28 See *Report of the Board Appointed to Enquire into, and Report upon, the Present Condition and Management of the Coranderrk Aboriginal Station*, 1882; Barwick, *Rebellion at Coranderrk*; Lydon, *Eye Contact*.

29 See Jane Lydon's analysis in *Eye Contact*.

30 Allan McEvey, "Le Souef, Albert Alexander Cochrane", in Douglas Pike (ed.), *Australian Dictionary of Biography*, vol. 5 1851–1890 (Parkville: Melbourne University Press), 1974, pp 80–81.

31 See Albert A.C. Le Souef's unpublished *Personal Recollections of Early Australia*, Le Souef Family Archives, Australian Manuscripts Collection, State Library of Victoria.

32 Albert A.C. and Caroline Le Souef, *Le Souef Box* (1860s), decorated box and miniature weapons, ink on wood, 15.5 (h) × 102 (w) × 15 (d) cm., Registration no. X 75992, Museum Victoria.

33 For a reading of this object and the narratives depicted by Caroline on its exterior, see Paul Fox's essay "Sweet Damper and Gossip" in the exhibition catalogue: Paul Fox, *Sweet damper and gossip: colonial sightings from the Goulburn and North-East*, exh. cat. (Benalla: Benalla Art Gallery), 1994.

34 Barwick, *Rebellion at Coranderrk*, p 317.

35 See Le Souef Family Archives, Australian Manuscripts Collection, State Library of Victoria; and, Douglas Pike, "Cotton, John", in Douglas Pike (ed.), *Australian Dictionary of Biography, vol. 1 1788–1850* (Parkville: Melbourne University Press), 1966, pp 249–50.

36 Fox, *Sweet Damper and Gossip*.

37 Vivienn Rae-Ellis, *Black Robinson: Protector of the Aborigines* (Carlton: Melbourne University Press), 1988, pp 191–2.

38 See Le Souef Family Archives, Australian Manuscripts Collection, State Library of Victoria, as well as Fox, *Sweet Damper and Gossip*.

39 For a full account of the early history of the Melbourne Zoo, see Catherine de Courcy, *Evolution of a Zoo: A History Of The Melbourne Zoological Gardens 1857–1900* (Auburn, Vic.: Quiddlers Press), 2003.

40 Leonard B. Cox, *The National Gallery of Victoria 1861–1968* (Melbourne: National Gallery of Victoria), 1971, pp 1–19; Ann Galbally and Alison Inglis, *The First Collections: The Public Library and the National Gallery of Victoria* (Parkville: University of Melbourne Museum of Art), 1992.

41 "...[I]t is also intended shortly to construct in the Gardens an old native Encampment such as the Blacks used to live in when the white men first arrived in the colony. The Council thinks this will a matter of great interest to many who have never seen or heard of such a thing; it will be the more interesting, as every detail will be faithfully carried out, even to the old weapons and stone tomahawks", Albert A.C. Le Souef, "Report to the Council" read at the Annual Meeting of the Zoological and Acclimatisation Society, 20 February 1882, *Minutes Book, Board of the Zoological and Acclimatisation Society of Victoria*, Public Records Office of Victoria; see also Catherine de Courcy, *Evolution of a Zoo*, pp 73–74.

42 "Steps will be taken in view of the intended International Exhibition to be held in Melbourne next year to make the gardens as attractive as possible, especially with regard to the fauna of Australia, which it is intended to increase. A varied and well arranged collection of the Australian fauna will have a great interest to European visitors. It is also intended before the opening of the Exhibition to re-establish the native encampment in the gardens, as such an exhibit will be interesting to the many scientific men who will doubtless visit the colonies next year. All the details of the encampment of the Aborigines who possessed the country where Melbourne now stands when the white man first arrived will be faithfully carried out". Albert A.C. Le Souef, "1887 Annual Meeting Report", published in *The Argus* 22 February 1887.

43 See the series of historical studies published by the Hotham History Project: *The Annals of Hotham* (North Melbourne: Hotham History Project), 1998–present.

44 George Rose, *Duke of York Celebrations, Melbourne—Fijian Soldiers at Drill, Encampment, Royal Park* (1901), stereograph, 9.0 × 18.0 cm, Pictures Collection, State Library of Victoria; George Rose, *Duke of York Celebrations, Melbourne. The Fijians at Drill, Royal Park Encampment*, albumen silver stereograph (1901), 8.0 × 15.0 cm., on stereo card 9.0 × 18.0 cm. approx., Pictures Collection, State Library of Victoria.

45 See for example the four photographs: The Argus, *Members of the Black Watch practising an Eightsome Reel for the Lord Mayor's Bush Fire Relief Concert* (1944), four gelatin silver photographs, each 17.0 × 24.0 cm, Pictures Collection, State Library of Victoria; The Argus, *Members of the Black Watch doing physical training and alertness exercises* (1944), four gelatin silver photographs, each 13.0 × 17.0 cm. approx., Pictures Collection, State Library of Victoria; The Argus, *Australian army on the move, marching* (1939–44), four gelatin silver photographs, 17.0 × 22.0 cm. approx., Pictures Collection, State Library of Victoria; The Argus, *Stripped for Aust. [i.e. Australian] sunshine U.S. troops enjoy calisthenics at Camp Pell* (1942), silver gelatin photograph, 20 × 26 cm, Pictures Collection, State Library of Victoria.

46 For example see *One of Melbourne's Best Sportsmen Responds to Empire's Call, Royal Park* (17 September 1915), silver gelatin photograph, Pictures Collection, Australian War Memorial, Canberra.

47 Edmund La Touche Armstrong, *The Book of the Public Library, Museums, and National Gallery of Victoria, 1856–1906* (Melbourne: Trustees of the Public Library, Museums, and National Gallery of Victoria), 1906.

48 Margery Ramsey, "Concept of a Library: The Melbourne Public Library", in Elizabeth Morrison and Michael Talbot (ed.), *Books, Libraries and Readers in colonial Australia: Papers from the Forum on Australian Colonial Library History* (Clayton, Vic., Ancora Press) 1985, pp 22–28; Bev Roberts, *Treasures of the State Library of Victoria* (Bondi Junction, N.S.W.: Focus Publishing), 2003.

49 Davis McCaughey, Naomi Perkins and Angus Trumble, *Victoria's Colonial Governors, 1839–1900* (Melbourne: Melbourne University Press), 1993, p 36.

50 Lydon, *Eye Contact*, pp 35–6.

51 Lydon, *Eye Contact*, p 35.

52 Bill Gaskins, "Walter, Carl", in Joan Kerr (ed.), *The Dictionary of Australian Artists: Painters, Sketchers, Photographers, and Engravers to 1870* (Melbourne: Oxford University Press), 1992, pp 834–5.

53 See Charles Walter, *Portraits of Aboriginal Natives Settled at Coranderrk* (1866), albumen silver photographs laid down on panels to form a composite image, 101.2 × 146.8 cm, La Trobe Pictures Collection, State Library of Victoria. For an excellent analysis of this panel, as well as Walter's other Coranderrk photographs, see Lydon, *Eye Contact*, pp 1–33.

Index to Images

p 2 Artist unknown (Melbourne, Vic.), *The native encampment, Zoological-Gardens, Royal-Park* (26 August 1882), wood engraving, published by Alfred Martin Ebsworth in *The Australasian Sketcher*, 1882, Pictures Collection, State Library of Victoria.

4 Photographer unknown, *Melbourne. Zoological Gardens. Specimens of Aboriginal amenities* (1889), albumen silver photograph, 10.8 × 15.8 cm., part of the series *Reminiscence of à visit to Victoria, Australia, April 1889*. Part 1, Pictures Collection, State Library of Victoria.

— Photographer unknown, *Native fight* (1895), albumen silver photograph, 11.0 × 16.0 cm, photograph of a painting by Caroline Le Souef depicting a battle between Aboriginal groups in a bush setting; a plaque under the painting reads: "Native fight, Lower Goulbourn [ie. Goulburn], 1848"; date of copyright registration ascertained from Victorian Patents Office Copyright Collection (VPOCC) Index: Dec. 23 1895, registered by Caroline Le Souef, Royal Park, Melbourne; Pictures Collection, State Library of Victoria.

— Photographer unknown, *Corroboree* (1895), albumen silver photograph, 11.0 × 16.0 cm., photograph of a painting by Caroline Le Souef depicting a corroboree; date of copyright registration ascertained from Victorian Patents Office Copyright Collection (VPOCC) Index: Dec. 23 1895., registered by Caroline Le Souef, Royal Park, Melbourne; Pictures Collection, State Library of Victoria.

6 Photographer unknown, *A display showing an exact representation of an Aboriginal people's encampment in the Bushland exhibit* (1888), albumen silver photograph, Archive of the Melbourne Zoo.

12 Photographer unknown, *Melbourne. Zoological Gardens. Specimens of Aboriginal amenities* (detail) (1889), albumen silver photograph, 10.8 × 15.8 cm., part of the series *Reminiscence of a visit to Victoria, Australia, April 1889*. Part 1, Pictures Collection, State Library of Victoria.

14 Tom Nicholson, *Untitled* (2009), photography: Christian Capurro, digital photograph, 17.0 × 24.8 cm.

20 Tom Nicholson, *Photograph of a picture of a mummified head loose in a Le Souef family album* (2008), digital photograph, 23.0 × 18.0 cm.

Acknowledgements

Drawings and correspondence originated more than two years ago during my time as a Creative Fellow at the State Library of Victoria. I would like to acknowledge this programme and the support of the Library during this Fellowship, and I thank all of the Library staff who assisted my research, in particular Dianne Reilly, Shane Carmody, Des Cowley, and Madeleine Say.

I thank Auntie Joy Murphy-Wandin for her generous engagement with my work and for her support for this project.

I thank the State Library for permission to reproduce photographs from its Pictures Collection in this publication, and the Public Records Office of Victoria for assisting with my research.

For their role in the realisation of the first edition of this book, as part of the exhibition *Animism* at Extra City and M HKA, and for all of their work, I would like to thank Anselm Franke, Katrien Reist and the team at Extra City. In particular I thank Anselm for the extended conversation around *Drawings and correspondence* and his ideas on animism, a conversation which fed my thinking about this work. My involvement in the exhibition *Animism* was generously supported by an Export and Touring Grant from Arts Victoria, and I would like to thank Arts Victoria and, in particular, Amanda Browne.

I would also like to thank: Anna Schwartz Gallery, and specifically Anna Schwartz and Sarah Ritson for their constant work and energy; Christian Capurro for his contribution to the work, through his photography and his insights on the drawings; my colleagues at the Faculty of Art & Design for their collegiality and support, and to the Faculty itself for the Travel Grant in June 2009 which facilitated the development of this work; Tony Birch for his friendship, his knowledge, and the sharing of this knowledge. I thank Roger Averill for his work as an editor and his thorough and perceptive reading of the work. As always, I have enjoyed the generous and skillful collaboration of Brad Haylock, whose engagement, deftness and hard work on the design of this book is gratefully acknowledged, along with his unfailing good humour. I thank my family for their love and support, especially my parents Mary and Peter, my three children, Luci, Jean and Joseph, and my partner Clare Land (whose knowledge and love fed this work in equal measure).

I would like to acknowledge the Wurundjeri as the original owners of the land on which I work and live. This acknowledgment involves an understanding that the legacy of invasion is ongoing and remains unresolved legally and morally.

—Tom Nicholson

Drawings and correspondence

Tom Nicholson

www.tomn.net

Second edition 2011
ISBN: 978-0-9807536-7-7

Published by Surpllus Pty Ltd
Melbourne, Australia
www.surpllus.com

Design: Brad Haylock
Editor: Roger Averill

Typeset in Galaxie Copernicus and Akzidenz Grotesk
Printed by BPA Print Group, Melbourne

Tom Nicholson is represented by Anna Schwartz Gallery. He is a Lecturer in Drawing in the Faculty of Art & Design, Monash University.

Brad Haylock is a Lecturer in Visual Communication in the Faculty of Art & Design, Monash University.

This second edition of *Drawings and correspondence* was produced for the solo exhibition *Drawings and correspondence*, Anna Schwartz Gallery, Melbourne, 10 August – 3 September 2011.

The first edition of *Drawings and correspondence* was produced for the exhibition *Animism*, 22 January – 2 May 2010, a collaboration between Extra City and M HKA, Antwerp. Tom Nicholson's involvement in the exhibition *Animism* was supported by Arts Victoria. *Animism* concept: Anselm Franke. *Animism* curators, in Antwerp: Anselm Franke (Director, Extra City Antwerp), Edwin Carels (Researcher, KASK/HoGent), Bart De Baere (Director, M HKA Antwerp). In Bern: Anselm Franke, Philippe Pirotte (Director, Kunsthalle Bern). In Vienna: Anselm Franke, Sabine Folie (Director, Generali Foundation Vienna).

SURPLLUS #1